WHAT IT MEANS TO BE
SERIES

PUBLISHER	Joseph R. DeVarennes
PUBLICATION DIRECTOR	Kenneth H. Pearson
ADVISORS	Roger Aubin
	Robert Furlonger
PROJECT CO-ORDINATOR	Sarah Swartz
EDITORIAL MANAGER	Jocelyn Smyth
EDITORS	**Ann Martin**
	Shelley McGuinness
	Robin Rivers
	Mayta Tannenbaum
PRODUCTION MANAGER	Ernest Homewood
PRODUCTION ASSISTANTS	Kathy Kishimoto
	Douglas Parker
PUBLICATION ADMINISTRATOR	Clare Adam

Canadian Cataloguing in Publication Data

Schemenauer, Elma
  Responsible

(What it means to be; v. 2)
ISBN 0-7172-2226-8

1. Responsibility — Juvenile literature.
I. Title.   II. Series.

BJ1451.S34 1987   j158'.1   C86-095058-1

WHAT IT MEANS TO BE . . .

RESPONSIBLE

Written by
Elma Schemenauer

Illustrated by
Steve Pileggi

Responsible family members do their share of the work.

It was almost dinnertime. Colette got the plates from the cupboard and started setting the table. Her mom was tossing the salad.

"Oh, look! It's starting to rain," said Tammy as she fed the dog. She ran to bring the newspaper from the porch.

Dad had just finished barbecuing in the backyard. "Lucky I finished cooking before the rain started," he said, coming into the kitchen with hamburgers that smelled delicious.

"It's a good thing we all pitched in to make dinner. It's much faster when we all work together," said Colette.

"Okay, the salad's ready," called her mom. "We can eat now, and then go to the movies."

Each person in a family has a job to do. Responsible family members do their work without complaining. They share the work as well as the fun.

Responsible people look after their pets.

Fergie the hamster was Tammy's special pet. His cage was in Tammy's room. It was her job to look after him. Usually Tammy played with Fergie every day. She also gave him food and water.

But then Tammy got a new bike. She was so busy riding her bike that she forgot about Fergie for almost a week.

One day Tammy saw that Fergie was huddled in the corner of his cage. He had no food. He had no water. He looked lonesome.

"Oh, Fergie!" she cried. Tammy cuddled her pet. Then she went to get some food and water for him. She promised herself that she would never again forget about her little friend.

If you have promised to take care of a pet, it is your responsibility to look after it. If you do not, the animal will suffer, or someone else will have to take over your job.

Responsibility means putting your toys away.

When Bobby came home, he usually put his
skateboard on the shelf where it belonged. But
one day he didn't feel like it. Hurrying to watch
his favorite TV show, he left his skateboard lying
in the hall.

   When Grandpa came to visit, he stumbled on
the skateboard and fell. Bobby ran to help.
Luckily Grandpa wasn't badly hurt, but he had
skinned his elbow. "I'm sorry I didn't put my
skateboard away," said Bobby as he helped
Grandpa with a bandage.

Being responsible means taking the time to put toys
away after you have used them. This helps keep
accidents from happening.

Being responsible means keeping your things tidy.

Hannah was cleaning up her room. She threw her stuffed animals under the bed. She piled her games on the shelf without bothering to close the boxes. She stuffed her clothes into the closet. When the closet door would not shut, she gave it a kick.

Then Hannah went over to play with Janice. In Janice's room, the stuffed animals sat in a neat row on the bed. The games were carefully piled on the shelf with every box closed. Janice's clothes were on hangers in the closet.

"Your room is smaller than mine," said Hannah. "How come there seems to be more room to play in your room? How come it looks so much nicer?"

Janice just smiled. She didn't say anything.

Do *you* know the answer?

If you put things away neatly and carefully, you help keep your home from looking messy and crowded.

Responsibility means doing your part.

Kim's mom was going to take Kim and her friends on a picnic at Sandhills Park. All the kids said they would bring something.

"I'll bring hot dogs," said Colette.

"I'll bring buns for the hot dogs," said Paul.

"I'll bring mustard and relish," said Mitchell.

"I'll bring some nice, cold orange drink," said Ryan.

At the park, Kim and her friends had fun playing tag on the sand dunes. They looked at their footprints in the sand. They even saw a raccoon's tracks.

After all this fun, everyone was hungry. The kids all helped Kim's mom unpack the picnic food they had brought.

"Whew, I'm really thirsty," said Paul. "I can hardly wait for a cup of that orange drink you brought, Ryan."

Ryan groaned. "Oh, no! I forgot!"

"But you promised you would bring some," said Tammy.

"There's a farm near the park gate," said Kim's mom. "Someone could go and ask the people there for some water to drink."

"I'll go if somebody will come with me," said Ryan. "I'm sorry I forgot the orange drink."

When you are part of a group planning something, try to think of a way you can help. If you forget a promise you have made, say you're sorry. Then try to make up for forgetting.

If you are responsible, you remember messages.

Paul's grandma sold houses. People often phoned her with important messages.

One day when Paul was at his grandma's place, the phone rang. Grandma had just gone to the post office, so Paul answered. "Please ask her to phone Mr. Johnson as soon as possible," said the voice on the other end.

"I will," promised Paul.

But then his cousins came over, and Paul went outside to play with them. They played baseball and climbed trees and rode their bikes around the block. Paul forgot all about the phone message.

The next day, Paul's grandma had to go to the bank. "Please answer the phone, Paul," she said, "and please don't forget any messages. Yesterday I lost the chance to sell Mr. Johnson's house because you forgot."

Soon after Grandma left, the phone rang. It was Ms. Knutson. She asked that Grandma call back.

"I'm going to remember to give Grandma the message this time," Paul told himself. He wrote Ms. Knutson's name and phone number on a piece of paper. He put the paper right beside the phone. Then he put an elastic band around his finger to help himself remember.

Just then the phone rang again. It was one of Paul's cousins, asking him to go swimming after Grandma got back from the bank.

"That's one message I sure won't forget," said Paul with a grin.

You can use little tricks to help yourself remember important things. For instance, you can write a note to yourself or you might even set a timer to ring and remind you.

Responsibility means obeying family rules.

Ryan and Janice were riding home on the school bus. "Do you want to see my rabbits, Janice?" asked Ryan. "You could get off at my bus stop today."

Janice really wanted to see the rabbits. But she remembered what her parents always said: "Let us know where you're going."

"Maybe I could come tomorrow," Janice told Ryan. "I'll ask."

When Janice got home, she asked her dad. He said it was fine to visit Ryan tomorrow. So the next day Janice got off the bus with Ryan. Janice and Ryan had fun feeding Ryan's rabbits, Hoppy and Blinky. Janice laughed at the way the rabbits' pink noses twitched.

If you are responsible, you ask for permission before visiting a friend. Your family cares a lot about you and will worry, if they don't know where you are.

Being responsible means obeying traffic rules.

Colette and Kim were at a garage sale. At the sale, Kim saw an old book that she really wanted to read. "I've been looking in the library for this, and I could never find it," she told her friend excitedly.

"You'd better buy it," said Colette. "Some of the pages are loose, but I think they're all there."

On the way home, Kim was already starting to read her book. Suddenly the wind caught some of the loose pages and blew them out of the book. Kim started across the street after them.

"No, Kim, come back!" yelled Colette. "Can't you see the light's red?"

Kim jumped back onto the sidewalk just in time. A big truck rumbled past, almost running her over.

When you are excited or in a hurry, it is easy to forget about rules like waiting for the green light before crossing a street. Such rules are made to protect you. It is important to obey them.

Responsible people obey community rules.

Arf! Arf! Jason and his big brother had a puppy called Nipper. A city law said that all dogs must be kept in a fenced yard or on a leash, but Nipper didn't like to stay in the yard. He barked so much that Jason finally opened the gate and let him out.

"Nipper probably won't go far," Jason told himself as he went into the house for a snack. But while nobody was watching, the little brown puppy trotted down the street to Mr. Martin's house. With a happy yelp, he began digging up the purple pansies and petunias that Mr. Martin had just planted.

"I'll call the dogcatcher!" shouted Mr. Martin, shaking his fist at Nipper. "This is the fourth time that dog has dug up my garden."

A few minutes later the dogcatcher roared up in a van with a big cage in the back. He scooped up little Nipper and drove him to the animal shelter.

Jason looked out the window just in time to see the van pull away. He realized he had done the wrong thing. When he and his brother went to the animal shelter, Jason paid his own allowance money to help get Nipper out again. Then he went over to Mr. Martin and apologized for letting the dog out. He offered to help Mr. Martin replant his flowers.

Community laws are made to protect people, property and pets. If you are responsible, you will obey them. If you make a mistake, you will admit it and you will do whatever you can to help make things right again.

Responsible people don't go with strangers.

One day Mitchell and Tammy were walking home from the playground when a red car drove up beside them. "Could I give you kids a ride?" asked the driver in a friendly voice.

Tammy shook her head. She and Mitchell both started to walk faster.

"You kids would probably like some ice cream," said the man. "It's such a hot day."

Mitchell shook his head. He took Tammy's hand and they ran to his house. When Mitchell's mom came out, the people in the red car drove away.

Most strangers are nice people who would not hurt you, but there are a few who might. That is why you should never go anywhere with a stranger or take treats from a stranger.

Responsible people know what to do if they are alone and away from home.

After Kids' Klub at the library, Tammy always walked home with an older girl named Andrea. But one day Andrea wasn't at Kids' Klub. Tammy tried to telephone her mom, but she got a busy signal. She waited a couple of minutes and tried again. Still busy.

Meanwhile, Mrs. Pickering, the librarian, was getting ready to close the library.

"I'm not supposed to go home alone," Tammy said to herself. "I'd better ask Mrs. Pickering what I should do."

"I'll be happy to give you a ride home, Tammy," said Mrs. Pickering when Tammy explained her problem. "What's your address?"

Tammy thought hard for a moment. "497 Kelsey Street," she said at last.

"I go right along Kelsey," said Mrs. Pickering, "so it will be no trouble at all."

It is important to know your own full name, address and telephone number. Then if you need help, it is easier for others to help you.

If you are responsible, you play safely.

DANGER—KEEP OUT said the sign at the building site. "Come on," said Paul. "Let's go play in there. The builders aren't working today. Nobody will stop us."

"No way," said Bobby, shaking his head. "Can't you see the sign? I'm not going in there."

"Well, I am!" said Paul boldly. He climbed over the fence and started walking across the boards that the builders had laid over a huge, deep hole in the ground. Suddenly he fell in. "Help! Help!" called Paul.

Bobby ran to the corner store and asked some neighbors to help get Paul out. When poor Paul was pulled out of the hole, he was wet and muddy. He had also skinned both his knees.

"You're lucky you didn't break your leg," said the storeowner. "You kids had better go home now. This is no place to play."

Responsible people pay attention to danger signs. They stay away from dangerous places like building sites, railway tracks and steep river banks.

Being responsible means taking care of younger children.

The babysitter called to Kim and Colette, "Girls, could you please watch the baby? I have to make some important calls for Kim's mom."

Kim and Colette took their game into the living room. But they were so busy with the game that they didn't notice baby Lee grab some matches from the coffee table.

Then, suddenly, Kim saw what Lee was playing with. "No, Lee," she cried, rushing over to him. "Matches are dangerous. Play with your crayons instead.

"Here, you can draw a nice picture on this piece of paper," said Kim, handing Lee some drawing paper and crayons.

Children can burn themselves with matches or even set a whole building on fire. You are old enough to know this, but a young child may not be. If you are responsible, you will stop younger children from playing with dangerous things like matches, knives or bottles of pills.

Responsibility means taking care of your things.

Jason and Bobby got baseball hats at the fair on the week-end. On Monday morning, both boys proudly wore them off to school.

When Jason and Bobby got to the schoolyard, everyone was trying to do somersaults on the grass. As soon as Bobby started somersaulting, his hat fell off. "I'll just put it here in my school bag," he said to himself. "Then it won't get lost."

Jason's hat fell off too. But he didn't pay any attention. After the school bell rang and everyone went inside, a strong wind came up and blew Jason's hat away.

He never saw it again.

Often it takes only a little bit of thought and time to take care of your things. Caring for your property is well worth the trouble. It means you will have those things to enjoy not only for today, but also for many days to come.

Being responsible means taking care of other people's property.

"We can build a model of a pioneer cabin at my place," Bobby told Jason. "My dad lets me use the stuff on his workbench."

The boys worked hard, measuring, cutting, pasting and painting . They were very pleased with the results.

When Bobby's dad came home, he was not so pleased. "Look here, Bobby," he scolded. "You left my scissors in the living room and my tape under the kitchen table. You even left the top off my can of paint. Now it's all dried out."

"I'm sorry, Dad," said Bobby.

"I'm sorry too," said Jason. "I know it was partly my fault."

"Come on, Jason," said Bobby. "Let's go clean up my dad's workbench. We'll put everything back where we found it."

If you use another person's property—and you should not do so without permission—you should always take extra good care of it. And always put things back where you found them.

Responsibility means taking care of your neighborhood.

Honk! Honk! Oom pah pah! It was a neighborhood parade, and everyone was there. In the parade were marching bands, baton twirlers, bright floats and even clowns with painted faces.

The parade passed by a park in the neighborhood where snacks were being sold. People weren't being careful with their potato chip bags, or with their hot dog napkins, or with their candy wrappers and pop cans. There was garbage all over the grass and flowers.

"What a mess in our nice park!" said Colette after the parade was over.

"People should have put their garbage in the trash cans," said Paul.

Your *environment* is everything around you, like the earth and sky and trees and lakes and streets and buildings. If you are responsible, you help keep your environment and your neighborhood clean.

Being responsible is important.

"We could clean up the garbage," suggested Ryan. He saw Mitchell, Tammy, Jason and Kim across the street. "Hey, come and help us," he called.

The other kids came over. Mitchell and Tammy started picking up all the pop cans. Colette, Jason and Kim picked up the potato chip bags and napkins and candy wrappers. "Here, put those messy things in the garbage can," said Paul.

Soon the park was clean and neat again.

Responsible people are good neighbors. They are also good family members and friends. If you are responsible, you will feel good about yourself, and other people will like you too. Here are some ways of being responsible.

- Pitch in and do your share of the work without complaining.
- Keep your promises.
- Obey rules and laws.
- Take care of your own property and other people's property.
- Help take care of others.
- Admit your mistakes and try to make up for them.

Printed and Bound in the United States of America